W9-CDU-994

BABY PORCUPINE

Published in Canada by Fitzhenry & Whiteside, 195 Allstate Parkway, Markham, Ontario L3R 4T8

Published in the United States by Fitzhenry & Whiteside, 311 Washington Street, Brighton, Massachusetts 02135

www.fitzhenry.ca   godwit@fitzhenry.ca
10 9 8 7 6 5 4 3 2 1

Fitzhenry & Whiteside acknowledges with thanks the Canada Council for the Arts and the Ontario Arts Council for their support of our publishing program. We acknowledge the financial support of the Government of Canada through the Book Publishing Industry Development Program (BPIDP) for our publishing activities.

Library and Archives Canada Cataloguing in Publication
Lang, Aubrey
Baby porcupine / text by Aubrey Lang ; photography by Wayne Lynch.
(Nature babies series)
ISBN 1-55041-560-3 (bound).—ISBN 1-55041-562-X (pbk.)
1. Porcupines—Juvenile literature. I. Lynch, Wayne II. Title.
III. Series: Lang, Aubrey. Nature babies.
QL737.R652L34 2005   j599.35'97   C2005-903737-7

U.S. Publisher Cataloging-in-Publication Data
(Library of Congress Standards)
Lang, Aubrey.
Baby porcupine / Aubrey Lang ; Wayne Lynch.
[36] p. : col. photos. ;   cm.   (Nature babies)
Includes bibliographical references and index.
Summary: For the first six months of her life, the baby porcupine never leaves the treetop as her mother cares for her every need. But one day the mother porcupine moves away and the young one must learn about the dangers of the forest on her own.
ISBN 1-55041-560-3   ISBN 1-55041-562-X (pbk.)
1. Porcupines — Juvenile literature. (1. Porcupines.) I. Lynch, Wayne. II. Title. III. Series.
599/.3234 [E] 22   QL737.R652L36 2005

Design by Wycliffe Smith Design Inc.
Printed in Singapore

BABY PORCUPINE

Text by Aubrey Lang
Photography by Wayne Lynch

Fitzhenry & Whiteside

BEFORE YOU BEGIN

Hello, Young Reader,

We wrote this book to share with you some of the adventures of a baby porcupine. The baby lived in a beautiful forest near a small town in Minnesota. We had so much fun following her around. She made us laugh many times. We always moved slowly and quietly so that we wouldn't frighten her. There were lots of biting mosquitoes buzzing around us, but we couldn't slap them because it would scare the baby away. Sometimes she let us get very close, and that was so exciting.

   We dedicate this book to our friendly editor, Ann Featherstone, for her skill and enthusiasm, and to porcupine researcher Dr. Uldis Roze, who taught us so much about the secret life of the porcupine.

—Aubrey Lang and Wayne Lynch

TABLE OF CONTENTS

The winter was long and cold. It was not easy for the female porcupine to walk through the deep snow to reach her favorite trees. Each night she climbed the trees to eat some bark. During the day she slept inside a small cave, where it was warmer and less windy than up in the trees.

Now spring has finally arrived, and the porcupine is a new mother. Her baby is three weeks old, and she is getting stronger every day.

The mother porcupine and her baby, called a porcupette, still use the cave where the baby was born in early May. When the porcupette was born, she was already covered with thick fur. Her eyes were open, and she had tiny sharp teeth. She could climb when she was just two days old. Because baby porcupines are very large, the mother usually has only one baby at a time.

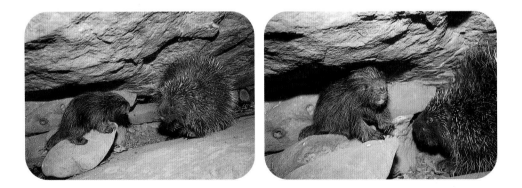

The porcupine is a slow, pudgy animal. To protect itself, it has many sharp quills growing on its back and tail. Quills are like toothpicks that stick out of its skin. A porcupette has quills even when it is born, but most of them are short and hidden by its thick fur. When the baby gets as big as its mother, some of its quills will be longer than your finger.

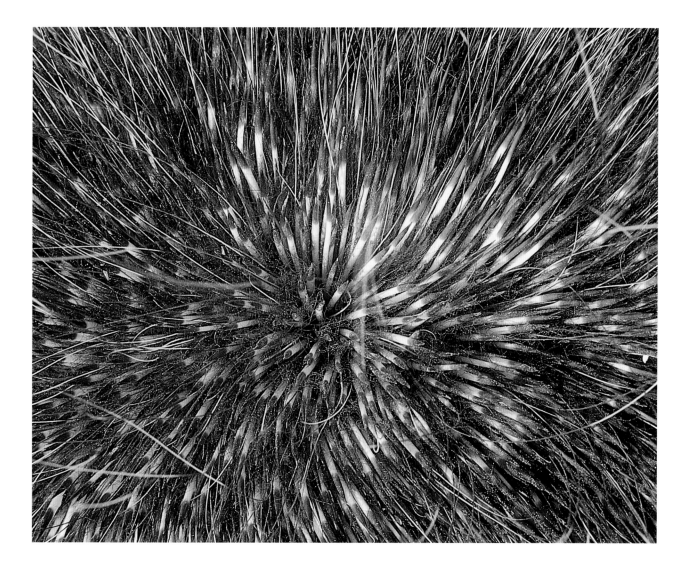

This morning the baby follows her mother to a big maple tree. The mother will spend all day sleeping high in the branches. The porcupette is not strong enough yet to climb such a big tree. She will hide in a small cave nearby.

A dead tree is leaning against the rocks on top of the baby's cave. It is a good tree for her to practice climbing. The bark is rough and easy to hold on to, and the tree is not too steep or scary. It is cold inside the cave, so the baby enjoys warming herself in the sunshine as she learns to climb.

When she grows up, the porcupine will spend most of her life in trees either sleeping or eating. To become an expert climber, the baby must practice, practice, practice. The bottoms of her feet are bumpy and rough like sandpaper in order to grip slippery tree trunks. She digs her long claws into the bark so that she won't fall and hurt herself.

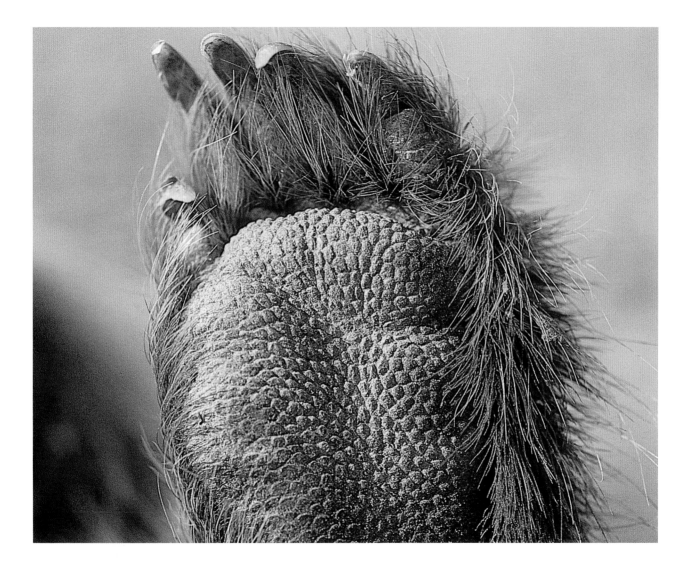

The porcupette drinks her mother's milk all summer long. But the baby soon discovers other good things to eat. She especially likes to chew the thin bark on small branches and the juicy leaves of raspberry bushes. She also likes to nibble on green grasses and dandelions. Her front teeth will continue to grow her entire life. No matter how much she chews, the porcupine's teeth will never wear out.

One day, when the baby porcupine is sleeping in her cave, she is woken by a strange sound outside. Thump… thump…thump, thump, thumpthumpthump. She is curious and heads out to see what is making so much noise. A big bird that looks like a chicken is sitting on a log nearby. It is a male ruffed grouse, and he is drumming with his wings to get the attention of a female grouse. The grouse is not dangerous. He's just a noisy showoff.

One morning the baby porcupine climbs high into an aspen tree—higher than she has ever climbed before. The branches are skinny and hard to hold on to. She gets scared and wants to go down again. As she turns around, she suddenly slips and falls. The porcupette bounces off a lower branch and lands with a thud on a big rock.

Luckily, the baby has no broken bones, but one of her front legs hurts. When she fell on the hard rock, she stabbed herself with the sharp quills from her own tail. The baby spends the next hour trying to get rid of the painful quills. She scratches at them with her claws and pulls them out with her teeth—this is something all porcupines learn to do.

A few days later, the sharp quills in the baby's tail save her life. A hungry fisher smells the baby and comes after her. The porcupette squeezes into a corner of her cave. Every time the fisher tries to bite her she slaps it in the face with her prickly tail. The fisher finally gives up and leaves with a sore nose full of quills.

The mother porcupine visits her baby every night to nurse her. After the fisher's scary attack, the baby follows her mother to a different area of the forest and finds a new place to hide. There are other animals moving around in the forest tonight. The baby has seen them before. She knows they are friendly, especially the deer mouse, the raccoon, and the saw-whet owl.

In the new part of the forest, there is a big river nearby. The baby learns from her mother about the juicy green plants that grow near the water. The mother porcupine isn't afraid of water, and she will even swim to reach tasty water lilies. Her quills, which have air inside them, help her float.

The porcupette will stay with her mother until early fall, when the leaves turn yellow and red. By then, she'll be half the size of her mother. She will have learned which foods to eat and how to protect herself. Before winter, she will move far away from her mother to a different part of the forest. There she can have a baby porcupette of her own some day.

DID YOU KNOW?

- There are twenty kinds of porcupines in the world, but only one kind lives in North America. It is found in forests, deserts, and mountains.

- The porcupine is the second largest rodent in North America. An adult weighs about 4 to 6 kilograms (9-13 pounds), but some can weigh up to 17 kilograms (37 pounds). Can you guess which animal is the largest rodent? It's the beaver—Canada's national animal.

- In winter, when snow covers the ground, a porcupine eats only tree bark. In a typical day, it will eat a patch of bark the size of a piece of printer paper. All porcupines lose weight in winter on this meager diet.

- An adult porcupine has two main ways to warn an enemy away—sound and odor. When it is threatened, the porcupine makes a clacking noise with its teeth. It also gives off a strong smell from a patch of skin on its lower back, which can irritate your eyes and make you cry.

- An adult porcupine has over 30,000 quills. But there are no quills on its face, belly, or the underside of its tail.

- A porcupine cannot throw its quills, but the quills detach easily when touched. The animal's chief defense is to flick its tail forcefully and drive the quills deeply into an enemy's skin.

- In spring, porcupines have a craving for salt, and this gets them into trouble with people. To satisfy their salt hunger, they will chew on axe handles and canoe paddles that have been soiled with sweat. They will also chew on plywood buildings and signs and on the wiring under vehicles that were driven on salted roads in winter. Because urine contains salt, they even gnaw on toilet seats in outhouses.

- Many groups of Native North Americans collected and dyed porcupine quills to decorate their deerskin clothing, belts, bracelets, moccasins, and medicine bags.

INDEX

BIOGRAPHIES

When Dr. Wayne Lynch met Aubrey Lang, he was an emergency doctor and she was a pediatric nurse. Within five years they were married and had left their jobs in medicine to work together as writers and wildlife photographers. For twenty-six years they have explored the great wilderness areas of the world—tropical rainforests, remote islands in the Arctic and Antarctic, deserts, mountains, and African grasslands.

Dr. Lynch is a popular guest lecturer and an award-winning science writer. He is the author of nearly forty titles for adults and children. His books cover a wide range of subjects, from the biology and behavior of penguins and northern bears, arctic and grassland ecology, to the lives of prairie birds and mountain wildlife. He is a Fellow of the internationally recognized Explorers Club, and an elected Fellow of the prestigious Arctic Institute of North America.

Ms. Lang is the author of over a dozen nature books for children. She loves to share her wildlife experiences with young readers.

The couple's impressive photo credits include thousands of images published worldwide.